T0162158

THE BOOK OF FRANK

THE BOOK OF FRANK

Wave Books : Seattle & New York

Published by Wave Books

www.wavepoetry.com

Copyright © 2009 and 2010 by CAConrad

Afterword copyright © 2010 by Eileen Myles

First Wave Books edition 2010

Wave Books titles are distributed to the trade by
Consortium Book Sales and Distribution
Phone: 800-283-3572 / SAN 631-760X

Library of Congress Cataloging-in-Publication Data
Conrad, C. A.
The book of Frank / CAConrad.—1st Wave Books ed.
p. cm.
ISBN 978-1-933517-49-0
I. Title.
PS3603.O555B66 2010
811'.54—dc22
2010027093

The Book of Frank was originally
published in 2009 by Chax Press

Designed and composed by Quemadura
Printed in the United States of America

9 8 7 6

Wave Books 025

well of course they're staring, we're very interesting.

[MY GRANDMOTHER]

FOR MY COSMIC OTHER,

ELIZABETH KIRWIN

AND TO FELLOW POETS

EVERYWHERE

ONE

when Frank was born
Father inspected the small package
the nurse handed him

"but where's my daughter's cunt?
my daughter has no cunt!"

Mother leaned from the bed
"this is your awful son Dear
your son has no cunt"

"why doesn't my son have a cunt!?
what has happened!?
what a WICKED world!
DARK!
and spinning
on its one
good leg!"

Frank hated the 9 miscarriages
kept in jars of formaldehyde

Mother burped each one

spooned peas against the glass

she rocked them all at once in her arms
no room for Frank

"you are too big for a jar my child
you will betray me the rest of your life"

milk pours from the sky

the countryside is comfortable
and burping

no one wants umbrellas

crocodiles snore on the white surface of the lake

Frank naps on the lawn
smiling

with tomorrow's sun
gutters will
curdle and
sour

Frank found eggshell
in his hair

"MOTHER!" he yelled
"why didn't you
teach me to dispose
of my shell like
other healthy young birds!?"

"because you're a boy!" she hollered

he flapped his arms and clucked

"STOP THAT!" she hollered

he pecked bugs off the ground

the rooster led him
behind the hen house

at the dinner party
Frank lost his fruit cup

he looked under the table

saw how people touch themselves

even at dinner parties

zippers stroked

knees re-acquainted with palms

his eyes clouded in jubilation

"but where is Frank?" they asked

while on their laps
the only answer
was a tiny
mysterious
violet

while Mother slept
Frank took her eyes

she told him never to do that

he saw the devil in every room
twirling his asshole
cooking small rodents
masturbating in Father's E-Z chair

all this through Mother's eyes

Frank was shaking
putting them back in her head

next morning
she marched into his room shrieking
"ONE OF MY EYES IS UPSIDE DOWN!"

Frank follows the crick
et
who   side
steps
every
rain
    d
    r
      o
    p

"this young
bird is trying
her wings

she's going to
defy gravity any
second now" Frank
said flapping

"I can figure
it out with
her I can
figure it OUT
WITH HER I
CAN FIGURE
IT OUT
WITH HER!"

Father was confused

which was Frank?

which the five
dollar bill?

the pornographer's smile
s   t   r   e   t   c   h   e   d
the room

after lunch
Father scolded
the five dollar bill for
jumping in the
pool too
soon after
eating

Mother was angry when
Frank accused his brother
of being a cartoon

"but look!" Frank said
"I can fold him
into airplanes!
I can chew him
into spitballs!"

"stop chewing and folding your brother!
he loves you very much!" she said

"then why doesn't he say so?"

"because

we can't afford a
screenwriter's fee"

"this daisy in my
mouth" Frank says
"is a snorkel
breathing
another
dimension"

one morning Frank's toast became indignant

smeared with butter it said
"you sir have no hope!
you will fail to see
the end of life
till you're half
pulled in!
you will suffer!
till you're all in flames
you will suffer!"

Frank ate him
with a laugh

Father masturbated across the table
newspaper headlines
in his left hand

Frank throws
pebbles into the
map of the
world and
readies
himself
to ride
new waves
of ruin

when Mother first grew
tentacles from her
shoulders Frank found a
path of ink across his
breakfast and went
to school sick

no one believed him

she arrived at school in a
long cape and burned the
principal with her eyes from across
the desk until she left with his apologies

her tentacles continued to grow with
a sharp smell of salt and fish

Frank followed a trail of ink to find
her wading in a black pool in the
living room
inviting him near her
nether beak

"when I die" Frank prayed,
"I will never return

if I must
it will be as
abortions
it will be as if I had not"

Frank ate clear around
the sleeping worm
of the apple

"any life saved in this place
is magic" Frank said
"it's life coming back to you"

Mother breaks Frank's paint brushes

forces his head
through canvas
"FRAME ME!" he shouts
"FRAME ME! take the copyright
from God! FRAME ME!"

every March Frank
loses his circle of friends

he's in the backyard

face in hands

surrounded by seven
carrots and seven
corncob pipes in seven
puddles of water with
fourteen eyes
made out
of coal

"oh the burden of
nouns no
verb can budge" Frank said

"like what?" his sister asked

"corpse" he said

"TOSS THE
CORPSE! LET'S
PLAY TOSS
THE CORPSE!" she yelled

"oh
you got
the corpse
moving" he said

"when will
you learn Frank
there is NO noun
a verb can't cure"

Frank hammers
carrots
all day

it works

the earth
can't
leave us

Mother made Frank smell her Bible
she knew he loved the aroma of fine leather

that carefully stretched
oiled skin

both Testaments went down
without the civility
of a fork

Mother sat by in her black scarf
pouring over rosaries and shame

"I'll eat them all for *you!*" Frank said
"I love *you* Momma!
I'll eat the Lord's Good Book for *you!*"

Frank met Huffy Henry sulking in a dream song
and zapped him
with the miniaturizing gun

Henry was kind of small anyway

Frank decapitated the
old boy with a pinch

tied his body on a
stick for a slingshot
and sent the little fucker's
screaming head up to
the great knee of Orion

"come any closer" Frank
warns Huffy Henry
"I'll pull you in
my sleeve!

anyone wants to know

the lump is just a
meal I'm digesting"

Frank's sister grew long blue feathers

she said it was worse than cutting teeth

she spent a month screaming in the cave
pushing them out

Frank would lie in bed at night
touching his own back

crying

praying it wouldn't
come to him

but the day his sister flew to the house
he stood by the window in awe
giant blue spread coming in across the lake

he heard the hunter's shot before she did

Mother knew where
the next war was
before Frank by
the colors they
made her
paint
the air
planes

the station wagon
lifted off the
ground

knocked down
flagpoles

chimneys

every churchtop crucifix in town

they landed
safely
in the drive

for years to come
Father turned the ignition

Mother and Frank
held their breath in
the back seat
fingers crossed

but it
never
drove like that
again

Father was drunk and
yelling "... AND RULE #9,
EVERYBODY DIES!"

upon hearing
Rule #9
Frank suddenly
forgot all
other rules

Frank grew crows for hands

it was a difficult childhood

at dinner during prayer
his crows flapped
excited in the name of the Lord
"FRANK! KEEP STILL!" Mother hollered
"did you wash your crows!?
did you wash your FILTHY STINKING CROWS!?"

when Father died
Frank was found
straddling him
his crows picking the seven
gold fillings

boulders
rolled
into the
yard

a pair of dice

Frank climbed the ladder
to find a five
and a two

he never saw the hand that threw them
swinging down to swoop them up

Frank saw
a giant eat a
park bench
with her
vagina

drink a
swimming pool
with her
vagina

"I saw her swallow the baby
and spit out the crib" Frank said

he tiptoed past her
snoring uterus one night
and heard a few familiar voices
cry out

Frank tries to ignore
the girl living inside
his mattress

she never shouts

never makes demands

he would talk about
the Mets with her
but he's afraid she
might never shut up

Frank can't
masturbate
as it is

airplane brings
Frank recipes
in Grandma's
head

"don't tell me it was
the wind!" Frank shouts

"THAT TREE
WAVED
AT ME!"

Frank found
a mirror
where Mother
cut him open
with her
words

Frank met
a woman on
the street who
looked like
Father in
drag

she was very understanding

agreed to smoke a Marlboro

arrange her crotch

say "I love you"
while avoiding
eye contact

when she removed a glove
Father's lovely hand
left Frank puzzled
quiet and
suddenly
corrupt

monkeys inside
Frank ascend
until his
bare
face is
covered

the family wore black in another room

fried chicken
lay across the
corpse absorbing
sins

Frank snuck a piece

licked each finger

belched

something inside him
spread its wings

something intending
to stay

Frank was
afraid they said
Special Circumcision
when they said
Special Circumstances

the rose
he lost was
just deeper
in his pocket

Frank loves his Coca Cola bottle

she loves him

he loves her fine lean waist

she loves his rock hard nipples

he shoves his cock in her little glass mouth

she cracks and
they're both in trouble

Frank's diary
returned
by mail
when he'd
lost it on
a bus

"Dear Boy come to Jesus"
penciled in the margin
for 108 pages

they thought it was funny
throwing darts
at cadavers
in med school

Frank laughed

they wheeled an old man in

a dart landed
bull's-eye
on a
testicle

Frank applauded

it was Grandpa

the sign read
HARMACY after
Frank shot
the P out

Mother's fine
china affects
her heart

when she
walks to town
Frank opens the
cabinet doors
and swings
a bat

he hears reports
of a woman who
died on the sidewalk
screaming "PORCELAIN!

SMASHED!

PORCELAIN!"

Mother's death
dripped
inside Frank

he covered his ears which
made it louder

his feet swelled
his ankles

shins

knees

would it stop?
would he burst?
drown?

after Mother
died her red
dress continued
baking pies

scrubbing the toilet

beating out the rugs

"I don't even miss her"
Frank said at
the dinner plate
meat caught in
his smile

they found
him in the
smokehouse
canned with
the beans
packed neatly
in the freezer

her red dress
snapping on
a flagpole
with no
wind

"would you sign
my book Mr. Poe?"
Frank asks the pile of bones
amidst shovels of dirt

"why certainly young
man" answers Frank in a
different voice

TWO

"this is your
captain" Frank says from the cockpit

"all passengers wishing to bail out
any time during our flight

it
is
too
late

I have shredded the parachutes to confetti
in celebration of our arrival"

Frank knows a
butterfly
who wonders
about her old
caterpillar
friends

Mother's longer arm
used to make a
tick tick ticking sound
moving in a circle
faster than the shorter arm

on the bus
a man asked Frank for the time

he stared at his watch
held by the memory of Mother

when he looked up
the bus was empty

his beard was

ten

feet

long

Frank pedals
his bike
to work

it's so marvelous
a ride he goes
home to
start over

a fortnight of this
he still doesn't
know he's fired

Frank woke once
four feet
shorter

a boy or
severed man

anyone who
can't see
he's a boy
at heart
is blind
to hearts

"I want to
move to
another
city" Frank said
"so long as
I don't have
to take
myself
with
me"

in the end

Frank
stuffed his
crotch before
the photographer
arrived

Frank is sad

her dogs like him
but she doesn't

he likes her dogs
but they are
forbidden to
visit him
without her

on the street
they bark for
Frank while she
looks away
pretending they
are not an
extension
of her joy

for love

Frank spoke softly
into envelopes
instead of
writing
letters

"I love us with the wig," Frank said
"it makes our voices change

you wear the wig
and ask my lips
to find you in the dark

I wear the wig
and track you
with my tongue

the wig uncombed!
the wig a fire of curls!
'the wig completes the head?' you ask
'the wig completes the head' I say"

Frank has
scissors

he makes
snowflakes
of your
panties

Frank was crazy to let her in

all the goddamn radios
and blankets
threaten
to play
her song
forever

Frank puts 4, 5, 6
sticks of
dynamite
in his
mouth

he lights a match

imagines the
gold it'll knock
out of his head

overloaded
on her kisses
Frank launches
out of his socks

defying the ceiling

which remains
unimpressed

in the Laundromat
Frank found
blueprints
for a cocoon
dropped from a
caterpillar's
pocket

"I must
try this at
ONCE! I must
try this at
ONCE!" he
chanted
marching
home

for Jonathan Williams

Frank is grateful
for the ride but
knows most trucks carry
semen stains

"Looking for these?"
the driver asks
pointing to
eager swimmers
long-since dried on
radio
ashtray
cup holder

"where these sharks
roll their
appetite" Frank
asks "am I
appealing

finally

to someone?"

on a blind date
Frank speaks with a
hand over his eyes

he's not afraid of
beauty it's just the 1st
time you see someone is
the 1st time

after that it's
the 2nd, 3rd, 4th
until you lose track

he orders a plate of peas
and smells them smells
them smells them

"aren't you going to
eat your peas?" Frank's
faceless date sighs

"no, it's too sinister how
one experience is quietly
consumed by the next"

she was exotic company
her mouth
full of mouse

Frank never heard a word
              his gaze
steady on the mouse
disappearing to reappear
with every syllable

              devoted
he prayed
to God she'd
marry him

but late in the night
she touched his hand

Frank recoiled
and realized
it was really
the mouse
in her mouth
he loved

though Frank
has never been
here before

she serves
him soup in
a wooden bowl
with bite
marks his
teeth
exactly
fit

Frank asked
to be alone with
her foot while
she hopped in
the kitchen on
the other

later
he won't
look her
in the
eye

something
wet has just
begun
to dry
on the
big
toe

she told Frank
"if I were
lightning I'd try
for that cup
of water about
to meet your
lips"

"you're an exhibitionist!" Frank said

"no, you're a voyeur!" she said

with four days to pay off
her handgun on layaway

                    Frank is
                   roped and
                    gagged
                    on the
                   kitchen
                   floor
                   counting

all the cats
Frank dropped
as a boy
from the 33rd floor
came leaping back
in one runaway lion

Frank hid in the closet
finger to his lips

the paw's
open
cleaver
swooped under the door

he lost
one damn fine shoe
and the
foot

in the diner a
woman Frank
doesn't want
to know asks
his name

he answers in
imaginary
vocabulary

"is that German?" she asks
"Russian?"

his lunch arrives

"oh!" she says
"this is pie!
can you say pie?

spoon!
say *spooooooooon*"

when Frank breaks into your house
he studies you with a flashlight Mister

you wake
in a wig
freshly painted
lips and nails
your wardrobe
switched
with high heels
and satin

you are frightened and scream
tho the hair on your chin
is all he cut off

a room full
of lesbian
ventriloquists
threw their
voices till every
part of Frank's
body told him
what a dirty little
hen he was

sunglasses
jump off
Frank's face
in supermarkets

leap into ovens

into traffic

Frank's teapot
wanted eyes

but they
leaked tears
of course

"I warned you!" Frank
yells "I warned you!"

with each dawn
pours another
sad
cup

the most intelligent hat
told its secrets to Frank's head

everyone knew it was the hat
but the king said no way
and the colors of achievement
draped Frank instead

the following year
the hat held its breath

Frank could barely spell his name

during the sunday service
the plate passed around with a clinking of coins

Frank was horrified when the plate came his way
catching him searching his pockets
finding nothing

they waited to see what Frank would do

free of money and full of faith
he offered himself
weeping
climbing into the plate of coins and bills

the congregation smiled
they touched him
as he passed from hand to hand

"we love you Frank" they said
and sopped his tears with bread
and ate the bread
and the bread was truly good

at the bus stop
the old woman asked Frank
"which bus are you taking
the #5
or the 12?"

"both" Frank said

May
flowers

Frank shuts
his legs

but

music

seeps

through

the cop
followed Frank into
the diner shouting "hey
Sleezebag! your shadow's
in the street
on his knees
blowing mine!"

Frank looks out the window
where a crowd has gathered

"yeah" Frank says
"they seem to be
finishing up

but no

they're just
switching
places"

"I'm not sure
which Jesus is
better" Frank said

"Jesus as Lord
gives me guilt
and shame to
need forgiving

Jesus as Toad
gives me warts
but is easier
to smash and kill

Lord or Toad?
Lord or Toad?

Lord

or

Toad?"

all summer
rumors of the chocolate man
had been around town

Frank found him on a park bench
melting out of his clothes
lifting a missing hand for help

Frank got a hard-on
from the sweet perspiration
and stroked his chocolate chin
with a hungry smile

the man shook his head no
but got his neck licked instead

Frank was on him
moaning over melting nipples
and biceps

the man shook his head no
Frank held the candy genitals in his hand
before he held them in his mouth

when he bit the cock off
caramel pumped steaming
in his face

the man died
shaking
his head
no

tell no one
Frank is
fat in his
thin coat

Frank shuts
his eyes in the
museum

he swears the room
is Andy Warhol

every direction he turns
smells of Andy Warhol

he opens his
eyes to find
da Vinci!
Raphael!
Michelangelo!

he runs to the
20th century gallery
to smell 16th
century Rome

Frank's favorite movies
are made in his head

he'll take your admission
if you insist
tho he never leaves
his one-seat
theater

bring your own popcorn

use the rest room
before you arrive

or hold it

Frank makes
sores on
the wall
with a
hammer

he kisses them

strokes them

"I'm sorry!" he
says "I'm sorry!"

Frank finds his
way home after
being lost

the gods said
they knew he
would find his
way home

"you didn't know that!" Frank
shouts at the sky with a fist

the gods said
they knew he
would say
that

Frank calls
"*BORING!*" out the door
and shoots
whoever
shows
up

THREE

"I'm here for the show" the man said
looking under Frank's shirt for the door

"I'm no theater" Frank said

a line formed

must he admit them all?

many had umbrellas

a blind woman
waited with
her dog

"it's gonna be a great show" someone said
"but when's he gonna let us in?"

Frank's tears began to fall

someone ripped his doors open

they filled him for an hour

the firemen were too late

Frank's house burned down

his neighbors circled around him

"you will lose everything
and everyone
you love today
Frank!

and you
deserve it!"

Frank was embarrassed in the bar
when his skin began to smoke

"hey man!" someone yelled
"do you need the fire department?"

everybody laughed

"no" he said with
a nervous smile waving
his arm to
clear the smoke
which only made it worse

"it will pass" he said

"it's just the
condition
of my Soul

it will pass"

Frank was fired from his job today

he wouldn't wear clothes

he said "but you hired me without them!"

"yes" they said
"but we thought you simply
needed time to find them"

Frank shuffled the cards

he noticed the Queen of Spades
with a small tuft of pubic hair
peeping out her robe

he watered her
till she sprung
a long vaginal beard

he whispered everything to her
EVERYTHING

but when the syphilis first appeared
Frank cradled his cock in tears

no blood flowed
so he gained little satisfaction
ripping off her head

Frank yawns "you'd never
know I lived for years
in the upper
left hand
bureau drawer
with a broken
spring and
corroded
batteries
in my neck
if I hadn't
just
said
so"

at the party
everyone traced fingers
on their bodies where they
preferred to have
cancer if they had
to have cancer

the host asked Frank
where he'd like to have his

"what a question!" Frank said
"I'd like my cancer right here"
and traced a circle
on the host instead

in
Mannequin Forest
Frank yells
"*TIMMBERRRRRRR!*

she's for Macy's

they need a set of children too

leave the axe
you can yank 'em by their necks"

Frank added milk to the
Instant Cowboy Mix and
herded himself into the
living room
                    mooing

the cowboy rode him slowly
around the TV playing a
lonesome guitar

when this was finally too
sad and boring
Frank ignored the warning label
and stirred a few more cowboys

his wife came home to
find him snoring
tied naked to the ceiling
bleeding from the rump
with a smile on his face and
a fresh brand upon his thigh

from the menu of
dead authors

Frank orders
Emily Dickinson's
breasts with
dumplings and the
braised thigh of
Anaïs Nin

his wife orders
Leo Tolstoy's
ring finger with
caviar and the
candied genitals of
Jack Kerouac

Kerouac's erection arrives
shimmering in gravy

"Mmmm" she says
nibbling the tip

Frank glares
and stabs
a breast

at the beautiful June drowning
Frank and his wife shout the
old woman's crimes
along with the crowd

"do you think
she can hear
applause under
water?" Frank asks

"I was thinking
your very thought" says his wife

someone nearby whispers "*she*
reads minds like a *witch*!"

Frank and his wife
sat at the dinner table

baked and glazed
the ham stood up

demanded prayer
clean hands
a kind speech in his honor

"DON'T LOOK AT MY LIFE FROM
THE CORNER OF YOUR EYE!"
the ham hollered

they begged forgiveness and
honored his requests

the ham grunted as their
knives pulled him apart
he wiggled and smoothed out
sighing on their tongues

Frank kissed the naked bone
over and over
held it to the sunlight kissing it

the bone purred all night from
the foot of the bed

Frank found
a list blowing
down the street
with his name
between
beans and
toilet paper

further
down the
list was
Elvis
between
cologne and
tampons

FRIGHTENED
Frank bought
beans and
toilet paper
to practice

Elvis was a natural
of course

"the table is flat!
the table is flat!"
Frank insists

his wife
with a sack of gold
and compass
sets out
on a hunch

many moons
and meals later
she returns
on his side of the table
her mouth a circle
her belly a circle
fingers arranged in the popular circle

"could I be so wrong?" he asks

the gypsy remembered
Frank's terror
of airplanes

she hid his
photograph
on board
a 747

he could be
seated at the
symphony

crossing the street

or fucking his wife

each time
the plane
takes off
his ears crack

he falls to the ground
fifty-thousand feet in his head

every night
Frank dissolves
into the sheets

not a man
but a stain

his wife rubs him
back to life with
her early
morning
vagina

he rises
            stuttering
            into light
more mineral
than man

one night
the dog
dissolved
with Frank

his wife rubbed
him back next
morning
      excited
      to find
Frank with child
at last!

at the doctor's request
Frank stopped shaving the chair

in a month it
was the most
comfortable
chair in
the house

Frank hands the
cowboy a wad of
tissues "these
contain semen
I produced when
thinking
of you"

the cowboy
sniffs them
and smiles
"thanks Frank
I'll put
them with
the others"

last month Frank
messed with her
tampon in
the trash

she knows he ate off it

his eyes said so
his breath

this month she
wraps it in tissue
stuffs it in her pocket

she opens the door

he is there
smiling
"give it to me" he says

Frank chops both thumbs off

he marches into the boss's
highfalutin' office

"I'm no longer primate!" he shouts
"I'm another species!

I no longer plunder and swindle!
I take myself from
this den of evil
a poodle!
a rat!
a lizard!"

"STUPID SPOONS!" yells
Frank "waiting
for me to
PUSH them
around the table!

bathe them!

stick them
in my
mouth
again
later!"

"is no one else
SICK of this
paralysis of
gravity!?"
Frank asks

"when I was a boy
I stepped into the sky
and I was a boy
not a surrealist!

part of the dream
is that you accept
your waking life as
part of the dream."

pig says to Frank
"this fence keeps *you* in *your* world"
Frank says to pig
"this fence keeps *you* in *your* world"
pig says to Frank
"this fence keeps *you* in *your* world"
Frank says to pig
"this fence keeps *you* in *your* world"
pig says to Frank
"this fence keeps *you* in *your* world"

with antennae
several roaches gabbed over crumbs

Frank wiggled his index fingers overhead
and eased into their conversation

he never expected to learn anything
never expected to fall in love

but since then
he's taken to cooking pots of garbage
and knitting tiny sweaters for the nest

they fill his bed at night

he reads Kafka's *Metamorphosis*
for a laugh

when they sleep
the room hammers the pendulum
of a thousand tiny hearts matching pace

"when I die" Frank says
"it might be as common as insecticide
but I have found my tribe"

"peas take
a deep
breath when
you open
their cans"
Frank
said

"Pea Activism
is your courage
and a
concealed
can opener in
supermarket
aisles"

it's no hat!
it's a marquee
on Frank's
head

children gather to read
the flashing words

TRUST NO MAN
WHOSE AORTA
LEADS TO THE
PULSE OF
THE CAPITOL

"*what does it
mean!? what does
it mean!?*" they ask

he says "if you hold
the snake away

from its
skin

there are
handbags"

one morning
Frank woke with
revolvers in
his hands

on the street his
neighbors painted
bull's-eyes on
one another

"they're waiting
for me" he said

tears filled his eyes

"good people
waiting
just for me"

everyone Frank wanted to kill
he let live

he sees
one make a
waitress
smile

"hey!" Frank says
"what GOOD
work I do!"

"we're 80%
water" Frank
says "20%
canoes
can't
ride"

Frank wrote on the envelope

FRAGILE! FRAGILE!
CONTAINS MY
VERY SOUL

he hid
in a bush behind the mailbox

saw the mailman read it

sneer

crumple it in his bag

weeks later
they pulled Frank
from the bush
    some
kind
   of
     rigor
mortis

Frank's skin turned yellow
orange and red
with the maple
oak and sycamore

his wife secretly
checked
the life-insurance policy

he arrived at
the doctor's
half-blind
brown and crackling

"it is no mistake
you have come to
my office thirty
stories above
the city" said the doctor

"relax by this
open window

Autumn's
ancient law
has no
escape"

bees fly from the
scalpel's incision

Frank's kidneys

liver

even
his heart
held in the doctor's hands
thrum with honey

Frank wonders
if the approaching
mouth of the
clock is opening
to swallow
or blow him
out of its
way?

"there's a small
bird I want to
save" Frank says

"give it a chance

but it's the size
of my heart
and I know
futility when
I see it"

from the pond floor
Frank watches bubbles
form constellations
on the surface

"you have no gills
you have no fins"
the bass
whisper in
his ear

"however we seek
another's weakness is
our tyranny" Frank says

he offers the bass a
sandwich laced
with hooks

Frank's spirit
floats out of
his body in
the restaurant

he reels it in
by its cord

at a movie
the man behind him
has scissors

Frank reels
nothing in

18 Self Help
books in 3 years
Frank is still
invisible

"can you see
the egg
pen and
empty notepad
behind me?" he
asks his wife?

"if I lie to you
I'll hate myself"
she says

"either way
you're still
invisible"

Frank remembers
shirts of buried generals
flying in formation
over schoolyards

blowing wasps from sleeves

for Bob Holman

after a speech about
other great maiden
voyages Frank smashes
the champagne bottle
against his house

he runs
inside to the
2nd floor window as it
pulls away from
the curb

"BON VOYAGE!
BON VOYAGE!" the
neighbors yell

Frank waving wildly
throwing kisses

Frank plays
chicken with
a freight train

it hits

his Spirit's
left standing

sure of
a miss

a ship whose sails
are Frank's first
diapers
mittens
and stockings
stops to pick him up

pins and
zippers of
other days
loosen

after his suicide
Frank returned to earth a
fancy-tailed goldfish his wife
bought at the pet store for her 3
Amazon piranhas

she held the tip of Frank's tail
and called into the green water
"Dennis! John! Carla!
SOUP'S ON!"

Frank is a
young boy
asleep in
ancient
Tibet

what you
thought was
your life is
really his
dream

he may
wake at any
moment

Frank rode
the dandelion seed
floating above
the street

AFTERWORD

I've been obsessing all year about CAConrad. For me, he's the poet who always changes the room he enters. The space he enters as a poet—on the page and in the room where he reads is invariably radically altered yet to specifically vague social ends. Yes he's queer. But aren't you? Conrad is undeniably a gay man who is generously reacquainting us in a quiet time (quiet about almost everything except the money—everyone's busy moaning about the money) with the wildness and inclusiveness of the original impulse behind the gay liberation movement, and even the implicit suggestion it carried then and even now that you, yes even fuddy duddy, uncategorizable, rich, poor, young, old you are welcome here. I'm thinking about his magnificent Frank poems which he wrote over the course of sixteen years then culled from a heap of them to produce this tight volume that is now tearing a hole in the aesthetic timeline of the poetry world. Conrad, a man in his 40s, hurtles towards us from a Black Mountain New York School In the American Tree Russell Edson Richard Brautigan Leonard Cohen Audre Lorde kind of present past. Like postmodernism itself the pastiche of his work proposes that all styles not only *apply* but *need* each other in order to explain the day. In order for us to fully exist in it. Conrad demands of his reader that we get in there viscerally with the awkward stuff. His first poem tells us:

> when Frank was born
> Father inspected the small package
> the nurse handed him
>
> "but where's my daughter's cunt?
> my daughter has no cunt!"
>
> Mother leaned from the bed
> "this is your awful son Dear
> your son has no cunt"
>
> "why doesn't my son have a cunt?
> what has happened?
> what a WICKED world!
> DARK!
> and spinning
> on its one
> good leg!"

This poem (like all the others that follow) is untitled. *Something* is in motion. The gyre of the wrongly gendered kid is spinning weirdly. No, Wyrd-ly I think is how you spell it, the gestalt of his opening sally. It's a weird emblem, the patch on the pocket of a wyrd family. It's Goth, Gorey, and again,

Russell Edson—himself an influential barnacle on the 70s heyday of the prose poem, of the arch surrealism that has since become sort of taboo except in some writing program where the progenitors still teach. Surrealism, for many today screams novice. Teenage. Cheap effects. But it gave us Bill Knott, it gave us early Codrescu and much of our connection to Europe and South America in the first part of the 20th c. in poetry. Surrealism implied among other things the disassociative and destabilizing states of sex. Like what *is* this thing I'm sucking on. Surrealism was part, I think, of a pattern of wildness that gradually became expressed in an ever more controlled and artificial way. Till like Stein says "it went away." I think it was replaced by technology. Surrealism reigned when poetry was cool, so it had to be "weird." It was a creaky stage, a late one, the Cheshire cat grinning just before the smoke of the writing programs filled the room. Now don't get me wrong. People have to work! And find time to write in a world where increasingly time only exists as a commodity. Not in that 70s way where time was a *space*. Conrad's taken a page from poetry's earlier carny moment and reinstalled it in ours where it's holding its own eerie glow. I mean what is it about a world spinning on its one good leg. Decrepit and demanding yet we can't help but also observe "the world's" agile perversity. You are wrong, the child is told. But as an epigram from the book suggests you are also very *much* worth staring at. A feeling prevails from the outset of *Frank* that is both disheveled and fantastic. Because rather than ever setting itself aright our attention keeps having its object replaced by the impossible proposition of the next poem. *Frank*'s is an entirely cinematic approach the way a film never stays still or wants to. It's a little bit like desire in its replaceable insatiableness. Yet (and wisely) the visual sameness of the poems in *Frank* are both grounding and bracing—if you flip through the book you'll see that the Frank poems are all about a page long—flipping it becomes a field of them. Haikus, almost.

Haikus—which are another dismissable item of poetry history. Hey we're doing haikus today in my workshop! Conrad's haikus are reports from an unfinished floating world—America, the family, hetero and homosexual deviancy lushly exposed, Disney-like. In one poem Frank's mother begins to grow tentacles, ones that are extravagantly dripping pools of ink. She picks Frank up at school in a cape (echoes of Di Palma's *Carrie*) then burns the principal with her eyes. The wild trail of events that follow in this tiny poem move Frank to this utterance:

> "when I die" Frank prayed,
> "I will never return
>
> if I must
> it will be as
> abortions
> it will be as if I had not"

What's most impressive here is how well-tweaked kitsch yields such quiet profundity. Maybe this is the site of his true distinction from some of the earlier surrealists. Conrad or Frank's own agony makes him unwilling to end his poem on an eye-fluttering and mysterious note. No corpse and key and uncertain direction mark these poems. Yet in no way is their surrealism tamed. It's more homeopathic. The tiniest differences here are telling. To return as *one* abortion would be vulgar, broad, the threat of an angry Goth kid. But coming back as a sea of them constitutes instead a community of loss. He's saying something theoretical *in poetry* through the mundanity of *stuff.* That cluttered place, the America of the malls and the thrifts and what's left on the sidewalk is indeed Conrad's academy. He's a connoisseur. He's like a PhD of stuff. An inspirational speaker of it. And he knows it.

> Frank ate clear around
> the sleeping worm
> of the apple
>
> "any life saved in this place
> is magic" Frank said
> "it's life coming back to you"

The sleeping worm of course is cartoony. Saturday morning type fun. But is "life coming back to you" that. In concert with the circular motion of the eating in the first stanza it's a mannered arrival at a simple feeling of awe, a visual

mitzfeh, a gift. The gift is that it *seems* so easy—is a cartoon
—makes it simple like Charlie Chaplin is simple. Maybe I
only think of Creeley and Lucille Clifton as two poets so
good at making the profound look easy. Each return visit to
these poems confirms this effect, since they always yield a lit-
tle more. These pop conflations seem to me to be the poems
of a contemporary master.

> Mother breaks Frank's paint brushes.

This is the first line of the next poem after the worm one. In
a public reading the one before would have extracted a quiet
ooh from a poetry audience. He made a bump in the air. The
atmosphere is now strangely dewy. Then he follows it up like
this:

> Mother breaks Frank's paint brushes.
>
> forces his head
> through canvas
> "FRAME ME!" he shouts
> "FRAME ME! take the copyright
> from God! FRAME ME!"

Is this funny. I think we're talking about family violence.
Whether a painting was actually busted or not—or a brush.
The casual destruction of childhood creativity in families of
all classes, and the casual and monstrous destruction of that

deeper art in a child which is the self, that space of pure orig-
inality, that's the real subject here. To address that Conrad
has inverted the meanings of "frame," "copyright" and
"God," driving over them back and forth, hurting every-
thing in order to dredge up freshly the reality of child abuse
while foisting on the reader the sensation of hearing one
time, many times, all the time that *you* don't matter. You
can't *make* or exist, that you can't *be*. You just aren't there.
This kind of Werner Herzog screaming to God is a demand
for the most primary honorific of having a name, a frame—
access to a sense of self in the world. Religion gets sneered at
by artists and intellectuals I think because there's so little
understanding (among those of us who have escaped, kind
of) of how God is finally the only institution many humans
can imagine themselves being witnessed by. Only prayer is
offered in the end to the poor—and the rich too I believe. If
we want people to imagine themselves freer than that then
we must take them (in some manner) out of their homes, and
schools and speak to them in *abling* language. Would that not
be poetry. Can it be. Poetry that steps out of the academy (or
never stepped in) generally tends to access that function.
"Frank" is an ardent howl. In elegant six, and eight and
twelve line bursts.

And let's talk for a moment specifically about gender.
There's a scarlet (meaning bloody, not erotic) even scary
feminist consciousness operative here.

Frank tries to ignore
the girl living inside
his mattress

she never shouts

never makes demands

he would talk about
the Mets with her
but he's afraid she
might never shut up

Frank can't
masturbate
as it is

I call it feminism, even outrageous feminism at work here simply because he *sees* her. Because the girl simply is. I might contrast this poem with the work of Tony Oursler, a video artist who makes mannequins with blank faces for his installations and places them under toppling couches then shoots a moving human face onto the blank oval of the dummy. She'll be screaming and whining and emitting plaintive cries. Sometimes his figures are men, but it's women mostly. There's this commonplace in male art where the gimmick of monstrosity is usually enacted by a female form. I guess cause that's who he's looking at mostly. *Not men*. But, really?

I mean that's the story that generally gets told. It's just the male gaze going on here. Nothing else. So when men work with men, and share their ideas with each other they're not looking. When they learn from other men it *all* takes place in the realm of the invisible. Just like in sports. I find that entirely unbelievable.

I'm saying what's different here is that CAConrad includes himself (the Frank character) in the performance. And he knows she's there. He's admitting that he is unwilling to endure her. When he imagines talking to her about the Mets I think he's suggesting that he knows he probably *should* perform masculinity "for" the girl. That's his job. But is he a man. That comes into question here. And what's acknowledged is that he has his own tawdry (or life giving, perhaps) desires and he is not willing to forgo them in an exchange with her. Because she might never shut up. That's the main problem. He knows just how monstrous she is. (Which as a woman I am weirdly honored by.) Though her monstrosity interferes with his needs. He's probably gay, this narrator. I'm taking that from his own awareness of masculinity as performance. He wants to jerk off that's all. And she will ruin it. I also mention gayness here because the Frank poems are a triumph of multi-positionality.

These are not men's poems, any more than they are women's poems. They're not straight poems any more than gay ones. I was giving him props for this in the beginning of this in a celebratory "opening the bar" kind of way but this is what I mean. The writer is male, and the writer is homosexual. And the writer comes it seems clear from a less than privileged background. But the scope of the book includes so many kinds of ventriloquized selves, an abundant puppetry. Like that field of haikus waving. An active and morphing fictionality amends, abets and broadens the scope of the poetry inside "Frank" and even out there or here where we live.

I imagine a kind of reader assigning to "Frank" one position: queer, weird, funny because I think we are urged to read narrower and narrower all the time. So that in taking a variety of positions one ironically allows the reader the opportunity to pick the weirdest one as the "true" position of the author. And dismiss it as that. Because the demand to write middle class work in a failing empire apparently overrides all other concerns and unless it's clear that we laugh at the other, or have judiciously picked one (other) as people generally do in fiction and carefully stick with that mask for the entire ride, then you leave yourself wide open to the lowest sort of critique posing as high. Imagine Whitman having to limit himself to one of the above, or below. It's our good fortune especially at this moment of quiet cultural crisis to have this marvelous book by CAConrad—one following Whitman and Stein and Allen Ginsberg who came to us all horny and abundant in their different ways demanding that he or she be construed as *all* men.

pig says to Frank
"this fence keeps *you* in *your* world
Frank says to pig
"this fence keeps *you* in *your* world"
pig says to Frank
"this fence keeps *you* in *your* world"
Frank says to pig
"this fence keeps *you* in *your* world"
pig says to Frank
"this fence keeps *you* in *your* world"

In Conrad's world the parameters are unknowable because that is the scary and real nature of our time. In piecing together, configuring and releasing his extreme miniatures—agonized fables, poems about America. CAConrad includes us all in the enormous outside of his heart. Which is the world in *all* its possibility.

EILEEN MYLES

ACKNOWLEDGMENTS

Much respect and gratitude to Charles Alexander of Chax Press, where the first edition of this book was printed. That edition was the recipient of the 2009 Gil Ott Book Award, as chosen by Nathaniel Mackey, Myung Mi Kim, and Eli Goldblatt.

Many thanks to the editors of the magazines where these poems first appeared: *Abraham Lincoln*, *American Writing*, *Animal Farm*, *Apiary Magazine*, *Bern Porter International*, *Blank Gun Silencer*, *Bombay Gin*, *BOTH/BOTH*, *Chiron Review*, *COCK NOW!*, *Creative Disposal*, *the dariens*, *Detumescence*, *Exquisite Corpse*, *Free Lunch*, *FUCKUPS*, *Indigest*, *Iota*, *Joss*, *KNOCKOUT!*, *LOVELESS*, *The Lower Half*, *Mad Cow*, *mind the sun you pig*, *No Restraints*, *Open 24 Hours*, *Oyster Boy Review*, *Painted Bride Quarterly*, *Poetry Motel*, *Range*, *Shrike*, *Small Town*, *Smalls*, *Snow Monkey*, *South 666 Bitch*, *Strange Horizons*, *Tameme*, *the tiny*, *Thumbnail*, *Torch*, *the Transcendentalist*, *Wobbling Roof*, *Zipperfucked*.

Some of these poems also appeared as limited edition broadsides. Many thanks to the editors of *BEST FUCKING*

FRIENDS PRESS, *48th Street Press*, and the staff at The Kelly Writers House.

Some of these poems appeared as a chapbook titled *Frank* (Insight to Riot Press), as well as a second, smaller chapbook titled *F* (Mooncalf Press). Thanks to the editors.

Thanks to the Berlin poet Holger, and to Jonas Slonacker and Sigrid Mayer for translating some of these poems into German. And to Carrie Hunter for publishing those translations as a bilingual chapbook on her Ypolita Press label, titled "The Frank Poems."

Thanks to Joshua Beckman, Ryan Eckes and Frank Sherlock for the close reading and editing for this new edition.

Thanks to Eileen Myles for her close reading and generous essay for this edition.

Thanks to *BOMB Magazine Podcast* host and editor Luke Degnan.

Thanks to Joe Milford of *The Joe Milford Poetry Show* online.

Thanks to members of the band IDEAS ARE BIRDS— Victor Korvera, Veronika Sweet, David Gould, and Ben Malkin—for inviting me to read from this book in a recording session.

Thanks to Dwaine for his rap song "The Choice Dear Frank."

Thanks to Scotty Leitch for his punk rock song "Frank Song."

Thanks to The Absinthe Drinkers for their musical *Songs from Under the Bed*, also included on their CD *One Cell, One Love*, the song *"No Room for Frank"* (TheAbsintheDrinkers .com).

Thanks to Laura Lynn Farwell for her short film of some of these poems.

A selection of these poems exist as MP3 files read by the author on *PENNSOUND* thanks to Michael Hennessey and Charles Bernstein (CAConradMP3.blogspot.com).

Thanks to Penn Book Center for including some of these poems in their Poem of the Day.

Love and gratitude to Charlie Wright, Joshua Beckman, Matthew Zapruder, Brandon Shimoda, Heidi Broadhead, and everyone else who makes WAVE poetry so amazing!

Love and gratitude to Tom Meyer, Jeremy Halinen, and the late Jonathan Williams of The Jargon Society. Jonathan encouraged me to keep writing this book, and to not rush, to let it cook, and make it be the best it can be.

Love and gratitude to Eileen Myles, Frank Sherlock, Magdalena Zurawski, Molly Russakoff, Zoe Strauss, Anne Waldman, Bernadette Mayer, Dorothea Lasky, Thom Donovan, Ryan Eckes, Anselm Berrigan, Rauan Klassnik, Joseph Massey, Tara Murtha, Susie Timmons, Erica Kaufman, Stacy Szymaszek, Jason Brooks, Joanna Fuhrman, Carol Mirakove, Jen Benka, David Wolach, John Coletti, Alan Gilbert, Hoa Nguyen, Michelle Taransky, Sharon Mesmer, Vincent Ancona, Jack Krick, Laura Jaramillo, Ben Malkin, Kevin Killian, David Buuck, Juliana Spahr, Samantha Giles, Brandon Holmquest, Ish Klein, Janet Mason, Jim Cory, Needles Jones, A. D. Amorosi, The Divine Miss Jimmie, Alex Abelson, William Howe, ALL OF The PhillySound poets, and ALL OF The New Philadelphia Poets, and Nail (for her tattoo of "Frank knows a butterfly who wonders about her old caterpillar friends" on her left arm)!

Please let them know when the time comes that the author wishes to be cremated with a copy of this book (and some dark chocolate) to let the molecules mix with loving irreverence.